LISTENING to NATURE

LISTENING to NATURE

How to Deepen
Your Awareness of Nature

By JOSEPH CORNELL
Photographs by JOHN HENDRICKSON

Dawn Publications
14618 Tyler Foote Road
Nevada City, CA 95959
U.S.A.

Exley Publications, Ltd.
16 Chalk Hill
Watford, Herts, WD1 4BN
U.K.

Cover photograph by John Hendrickson

ISBN: 0-916124-35-5 (Dawn Publ.)
        1-85015-094-X (Exley Publ., hardcover)
        1-85015-095-8 (Exley Publ., paperback)

CONTENTS

TO MY PARENTS,
*who instilled a love for nature
in my brothers and me by sharing
many places of natural beauty with us.*

and

TO MY WIFE,
*for her clarity,
joy and friendship.*

Listening to Nature

RECENTLY, at the end of one of my nature awareness workshops, we were sitting beside a trail, quietly enjoying the stillness of the surrounding forest. We had just finished doing several nature activities that had enabled us to become calm and receptive. The calling birds, the wind streaming overhead, and the play of light and shadows on the forest floor drew our attention to the beauty of the present moment.

The stretch of the trail where we had paused is one of the most beautiful and popular parts of the park. When other hikers walked by, our group was struck by the contrast between our experience and that of most of the other people. Long before their approach, we heard them discussing such topics as work, politics and restaurants. Later, we reflected on how easy it is to walk through the wilderness so engrossed in our own private concerns or in conversation that we notice little of our surroundings.

I once demonstrated this to a group of twenty-five teachers in Canberra, Australia. I asked them to look at a beautiful tree as long as they were able to, and to raise their hands when their attention wandered from the tree and drifted to other thoughts. In only six seconds, every

hand was raised. They were amazed to discover how restless their minds were.

To experience and understand the world around us, it's essential that we focus our minds. For only by listening deeply, with a quiet mind, can we ever fully experience nature.

I am reminded of a story told to me by a friend. He was standing one night on a hotel balcony in Mexico, enjoying the city lights spread before him, when suddenly a power failure plunged everything into darkness. Everything, that is, but the stars, which he had not even noticed a moment before. He reflected on how, just as the closer glow of the city had overpowered the subtler light of the heavens, so our own restless thoughts overpower our perceptions of the subtle beauties of nature—and the subtle aspects of our own lives.

Yet, after spending many days in the wilderness, people notice that their problems and distractions have faded away. Everything they see, hear, and smell becomes extraordinarily beautiful, in their freed and focused attention. In this intensity of experience they may feel a deeper calmness, joy, and aliveness than ever before.

Few of us live in wilderness areas, so we're not often able to stay in the wilds long enough to have these kinds of experiences; but all of us can become more receptive to the aspects of nature we *do* experience. Because, it isn't where we are that's important—rather, it's how deeply *we* are able to see and experience, no matter where we are.

Thoreau said, "All wisdom is the reward of a discipline, conscious or unconscious." Because the "wisdom" of nature awareness doesn't come to us automatically, I've gathered uplifting thoughts and activities that all of us can use as conscious, rewarding "discipline," to increase our ability to tune into nature.

Several years ago, while I was living in a cabin in the Sierra Nevada mountains of northern California, I wrote a poem, "The Birds of the Air" (see Day 6), to recall my experiences of oneness with all life. I'd walk in the woods every day, repeating the poem over and over, as a way to cultivate love for the earth. This became my steady practice, and when the summer ended and I toured to teach nature awareness, I always took time before each workshop to sit or walk quietly, repeating the poem to attune myself to the inspiration flowing from nature. The more deeply I entered into the spirit of the poem, the more inspiration and success I experienced in my workshops.

I also studied the lives of famous naturalists and nature mystics over the years, and again, because I found so much inspiration in their words and experiences, I began to collect inspiring passages from their written and spoken words.

Listening to Nature is the result of twenty years effort of discovering, refining and sharing universal principles and techniques of nature awareness. The most popular and uplifting quotations and activities I've used in my workshops are presented here. I hope you'll draw inspiration from them and share them with friends.

May you always walk the earth in love and beauty.

JOSEPH CORNELL

LISTENING TO NATURE is arranged as a monthly diary that can be used again and again. Each day's pages offer an inspiring quotation, often with an activity or explanation to help you translate the idea into personal experience.

This book was designed to offer you the insights and approaches of many lovers of nature, just for your inspiration. I hope you will also enjoy reading the stories and explanations that accompany the quotations. They are meant to enhance the quotations and make each one more applicable to your daily life.

But my real goal in writing this book—and my hope for you—is that you'll use it as an exercise book. Each day offers a "discipline," you might say, that can open you to nature in a way that may be new to you. Even if the activity or thought is not new for you, you'll benefit from consciously focusing on that one thought for the day.

A sage once said, "As we think, so we become." Some of the quotations may be used as affirmations. You can read and repeat the quotation to yourself in the morning, then often throughout the day, to help you deeply absorb its meaning.

You do not have to be in the wilderness to do these activities. In fact, you can do many of them while driving or walking to work. As you use the activities more and more, your receptivity will increase, and you'll begin to see beauty in the most common things.

When you're outdoors, flip through the book to find quotations and activities that inspire you. With the help of these passages and activities, you'll find it easier to absorb the beauty and serenity of natural places.

*"Come forth
into the light of things.
Let Nature be your
teacher."*

—WILLIAM WORDSWORTH

"*I*f you love it enough, anything will talk with you."

—GEORGE WASHINGTON CARVER

While you're outdoors, observe an animal closely. Follow it as it moves. See how nature has expressed itself uniquely in this animal. Become quiet within your mind, so that you can become sensitively aware of the animal's essence. Mentally offer your appreciative thoughts to the animal. Listen.

With deer and other animals, it helps to establish your friendly intentions by speaking frequently and soothingly, so that they always know where you are and get used to your presence. As you come closer, don't walk straight at them, but go off a little to the side. Also, don't stare directly at them. Thus you'll give the impression that you're only passing through and mean no harm.

In time, they'll accept you, and will even look to see if you're following as they move on. A friend of mine, Denny Olson, spent several hours using these techniques with three deer he encountered in a wilderness meadow. The deer eventually accepted him so completely that, when they bedded down for the night, and each one took a different direction to watch for danger, they left the fourth direction for Denny!

You can also do this activity with smaller animals, such as butterflies and squirrels.

"One's happiness depends less on what he knows than on what he feels."

—LIBERTY HYDE BAILEY

I knew an old farmer who often spoke fondly of the birds around his ranch. He didn't know their proper names, and sometimes he told us "facts" that were incorrect. I'm sure that any experienced birdwatcher would have discounted much of the farmer's wisdom.

But, how he enjoyed birds! I remember watching his wrinkled face while his eyes filled with delight, as he gazed up at flocks of swans and geese passing overhead. He became so totally absorbed in their shifting formations and clamouring cries that it took him a few moments to come back to himself.

Because of his joy and absorption in the birds, I've always felt he knew the right approach and had gained more from his bird study than had many a more scientific observer.

Go for a walk in the wild. Avoid categorizing the things you see; instead, focus on feeling a kinship with everything you see. Look at everything as though you are seeing it for the first time, with the eyes of a child, fresh with wonder.

THREE

"The care of rivers is not a question of rivers, but of the human heart."

—TANAKA SHOZO

With love comes understanding and the motivation for right action.

"*I* *think I could turn and live with the animals, they are so placid and self-contained."*

—WALT WHITMAN

Still Hunting: There's a special thing that happens when we meet wild animals in the woods—a mysterious response in us that comes close to our hearts. The mood is even stronger when the animals are unaware of our presence.

Our presence in an area usually does disrupt the animals' natural activity, unfortunately. But the American Indians invented a way to get around this. "Still hunting," as they called it, involved sitting absolutely motionless and waiting for the world of nature to return to its normal, harmonious routine. Young people were urged to do this as a way of learning things upon which their very survival might depend later in life.

Choose a place where there are signs of animal activity, or that would seem attractive to animals. Sit where your profile is hidden by shadows, or broken up by trees, rocks, and other features of the landscape. Melt into the landscape and let nature come back to life around you.

It helps to approach the site quietly, and to wear clothes that blend with the surroundings. Sit for at least twenty minutes. Don't expect a caravan of animals to come parading by. (Though often I've been fortunate to have large animals come very close.) Your experience will be most enjoyable if you free your mind from expectations, paying attention to what you do see and hear: busy insects, singing birds, and breezes bringing the trees to life.

Listening to Nature **21**

FIVE

"With beauty before me,
May I walk
With beauty behind me,
May I walk
With beauty above me,
May I walk
With beauty below me,
May I walk
With beauty all around me,
May I walk
Wandering on a trail of beauty,
Lively, I walk."

—NAVAJO INDIANS

Go to a place of special beauty, near your home or wherever you may be. Walk and silently repeat this Navajo chant, feeling yourself responding to and absorbing the beauty you see all around.

SIX

The Birds of the Air

The birds of the air are my
brothers,
All flowers my sisters,
The trees are my friends.
All living creatures,
Mountains and streams,
I take unto my care.
For this green earth is our mother,
Hidden in the sky is
the Spirit above.
I share one life with all who are here;
To everyone I give my love,
To everyone I give my love.

Here is an activity that can be very helpful in awakening your own deep feelings for nature. Select a poem or passage that expresses your feelings toward nature. Or, better still, write your own, such as I did with "The Birds of the Air."

Go to a place where there are trees and frequent animal visitors, sit comfortably, and begin to repeat your selection. As you say each line or phrase, feel its meaning and project these feelings out to your surroundings. For example, while saying, "The trees are my friends..," from the poem above, feel your closeness to the trees. Repeat your selection aloud first, then softly, then mentally. Finally, put aside all thoughts and words, and sit quietly, enjoying the feelings they have created.

SEVEN

"*Simplicity in all things is the secret of the wilderness and one of its most valuable lessons. It is what we leave behind that is important. I think the matter of simplicity goes further than just food, equipment, and unnecessary gadgets; it goes into the matter of thoughts and objectives as well. When in the wilds, we must not carry our problems with us or the joy is lost.*"

—SIGURD OLSON

Mark Twain was once asked if he wouldn't like to go off on holiday. He replied, "I'd be glad to, if only I didn't have to take that fella, Mark Twain, with me." Like Mark Twain, we often take "that fella" along with us when we go outdoors for recreation. Our problems, worries, and other mental baggage usually tag along with us. Being so preoccupied with our internal world keeps us from feeling our unity with the natural world.

When you go out into nature, leave your everyday plans and concerns behind. Freeing yourself in this way will allow you to experience nature's cleansing and rejuvenating power.

Listening to Nature

EIGHT

"My heart is tuned to the quietness that the stillness of nature inspires."

—HAZRAT INAYAT KHAN

Find a quiet place, where you can be alone. Listen to the sounds around you. *Listen also for the silences between sounds.* When your mind wanders, repeat the above saying. It will help to bring you back to the present moment. I've especially enjoyed doing this activity in the quiet of the desert, and in the mountains in winter.

NINE

"You cannot perceive beauty but with a serene mind."

—HENRY DAVID THOREAU

Often, our minds are like the switch on a short-wave radio: when the switch is set to "broadcast," all we can hear is our own voice talking. We can't really *hear* until the switch is turned to "receive."

Similarly, a busy, chattering mind is always in "sending mode." The noise of our own minds prevents us from deeply experiencing and learning from the world around us.

When you are out in nature, be sure to take time to let your mind stop describing, analyzing, evaluating. Simply let it witness and appreciate what your senses bring to its attention.

TEN

Visualize that your mind is a pristine mountain lake. At the edge of the lake is a mountain ridge with its image reflected upon the lake's surface.

Imagine that your thoughts are winds that ripple the lake's surface, preventing you from seeing the reflection clearly, but as your thoughts slow down and the breezes cease . . . you see the image of the mountains perfectly.

To see and experience nature more deeply, always try to keep the lake of your mind in a state of perfect, unruffled calm.

To remind myself to slow down mentally in order to appreciate more fully a beautiful landscape, I often repeat a poem inspired by a visit to the Grand Canyon:

Let my mind become silent,
And my thoughts come to rest.
I want to see
All that is before me.
In self-forgetfulness,
I become everything.

ELEVEN

"The still mind of the sage is a mirror of heaven and earth . . ."
—CHUANG TZU

Stillness Meditation: I've often spent hours immersing myself in a landscape with the help of this exercise. It will help you see clearly, and so enable you to identify with and merge yourself in your surroundings. Your memories of natural places where you've practiced this meditation will be much more clearly defined. This technique also helps quiet restless thoughts and sometimes brings on a wonderful calmness.

First, relax the body. Do this by inhaling and tensing all over: feet, legs, back, arms, neck, face—as much as you possibly can. Then throw the breath out and relax completely. Repeat this several times.

To practice the technique itself: observe the *natural* flow of your breath. Do not control the breath in any way! Simply follow it with your attention. Each time you inhale, think "Still." Each time you exhale, think "Ness." Repeating "Still . . . Ness" with each complete breath helps focus the mind and prevents your attention from wandering from the present moment.

During the pauses between inhalation and exhalation, stay in the present moment, calmly observing whatever is in front of you. If thoughts of the past or future disturb your mind, just calmly, patiently bring your attention back to what is before you, and to repeating "Still . . . Ness" with your breathing.

This technique will help you to become absorbed in natural settings for longer and longer periods. Use it when you want to feel this calmness, indoors or outdoors, with eyes open or closed.

TWELVE

"*In climbing where the danger is great, all attention has to be given the ground step by step, leaving nothing for beauty by the way. But this care, so keenly and narrowly concentrated, is not without advantages. One is thoroughly aroused. Compared with the alertness of the senses and corresponding precision and power of the muscles on such occasions, one may be said to sleep all the rest of the year. The mind and body remain awake for some time after the dangerous ground is past, so that arriving on the summit with the grand outlook—all the world spread below—one is able to see it better, and brings to the feast a far keener vision, and reaps richer harvests than would have been possible ere the presence of danger summoned him to life."* —JOHN MUIR

No matter where we are, or what we're doing, the key to experiencing the heightened state of awareness that often comes to the mountaineer is to "keenly and narrowly concentrate" our attention. Mental disciplines like the Stillness Meditation are invaluable, because they help focus our attention and enable us to climb the inner summits of our minds. As our minds become free and clear, like mountain air, we experience everything around us with increased clarity and perception.

THIRTEEN

"*Man is not himself only . . .
He is all that he sees;
all that flows to him from a
thousand sources. . . .
He is the land, the lift of its
mountain lines, the
reach of its valleys.*"

—MARY AUSTIN

Expanding Circles: All of us enjoy gazing out across large lakes and fields, and other expansive landscapes. The Expanding Circles activity will greatly enhance your "gazing," by helping you focus attention more clearly on what you're seeing. Whenever I do this activity, I experience the great, harmonious sea of life surrounding me.

Expanding Circles works best if you sit where you have a panoramic view, and also an interesting foreground. For example, sit where there are flowers and grasses and perhaps a shrub close by, trees a little farther away, and a mountain ridge in the distance.

Begin by becoming aware of your body. Feel your feet and legs, hands and arms, spinal column and head.

Now, extend your awareness beyond your body just a few feet to the nearby grasses, rocks and insects. Feel

Listening to Nature   **39**

yourself moving and becoming alive in them. Try to feel that you are in everything you see, as much as you are in your own body. (Any relaxed effort at expansion, even if you don't feel you are really getting very far, will bring a surprising sense of broadened awareness and empathy.) Do this for a couple of minutes. When your mind wanders, gently bring it back to what's before you.

Broaden your awareness further to include the nearby shrubs and trees ten ... twenty ... thirty feet away. Feel that everything you see is part of you.

Extend your awareness out fifty yards ... a hundred yards ... to the distant ridges ... and into the vast blue sky.

All the while, keep the awareness of yourself in the closest things near you, as well as all the way out to the distant mountains and sky. Feel that you are in everything you see just as much as you are in your own body.

Ecology is the intellectual study of the interrelationships of all living things. Activities like Expanding Circles complement the science of ecology by providing a way for us to consciously affirm and intuitively experience our oneness with Life.

FOURTEEN

"*Here is calm
so deep, grasses cease waving . . .
wonderful how completely
everything in wild
nature fits into us, as if truly part
and parent of us. The
sun shines not on us, but in us. The
rivers flow not past,
but through us, thrilling, tingling,
vibrating every fiber
and cell of the substance of our
bodies, making them glide and sing.*"

—JOHN MUIR

Walking and Feeling Yourself in All:

As you walk, feel that everything around you is a part of you. Feel yourself in the trees, standing tall and firm. Feel inside of you the movement of their branches and leaves as they sway and flutter to the slightest breezes.

Become the birds as they flit from branch to branch. Listen to their calls and feel their sound resonating within you. Rise and fall with the ravens as they ride and play in the currents of air. Follow them until they disappear into the blue.

Follow the wind by the sounds and movement it creates as it flows through, around and over trees, meadows and rocks.

Feel yourself in every sound and movement of nature.

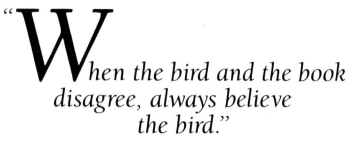

"When the bird and the book
disagree, always believe
the bird."

—BIRDWATCHER'S PROVERB

This humorous proverb stresses the importance of experiencing life directly rather than relying on secondhand information.

To observe birds close-up, you can make a sound that attracts many small birds, like nuthatches, sparrows, warblers and wrens. Simply repeat the sound "pssh," several times, in sets of four:

pssh ... pssh ... pssh ... pssh

Repeat three to five sets of this bird call, then wait to see what happens.

For the call to work, of course, there must be birds in the area. When you hear or see some birds, sit or stand near the branches of a tree or shrub before you begin to call, to give the birds a landing spot close by. Once the birds come, using the call periodically will help keep them around you.

Many times, over fifty birds have responded to my use of this call, even coming within a few feet of me. Once a mountain chickadee flew out of its nesting hole in a nearby tree and landed on my shoulder!

Listening to Nature   **45**

"*Folks wonder how I've kept so young. I'm almost seventy-seven and I can still go over a gate or run a footrace or kick the chandelier. That's because my body is no older than my mind— and my mind is adolescent. It has never grown up. It never will, I hope. I'm as inquisitive as I was at eight.*"

—LUTHER BURBANK

To illustrate the importance of spontaneity and discovery, Steve, a naturalist friend, tells this amusing story:

"I was leading a class of young children on a walk. When we got to a stream crossing, I started to show them crayfish holes, as I usually do. With a great deal of enthusiasm, I said, 'Let's kneel down and find out who lives in these holes along the bank.' None of the children responded. While still kneeling, I glanced behind me and could see that they were still standing, so with even more enthusiasm I said, 'Let's all get down and look closely—these are crayfish houses!' The children still didn't respond.

"Because the children were clustered so closely and I was kneeling on the ground, I could only see the lower halves of their bodies. When I turned around and looked up I saw all the children, perfectly motionless with faces turned upward, gazing at a large owl perched on a branch just six feet above us."

Steve laughed and said, "I'd become so used to showing children those crayfish holes that I didn't even notice the owl. I learned the importance of letting go of plans and of being more receptive to what's going on around us—like children are."

Cultivate the child within you by doing something unusual and fun outdoors. Climb a tree; wade through a marsh; run or roll downhill; call back to the birds. Having fun will bring out the child in you, and you'll feel a fresh delight and "at-homeness" in the world of nature.

"*If a child is to keep alive his inborn sense of wonder . . . he needs the companionship of at least one adult who can share it, rediscovering with him the joy, excitement and mystery of the world we live in.*"

—RACHEL CARSON

One morning, I saw my friend Carol walking very quickly with her little daughter Julia along a footpath near my home. Julia, who was only three, wanted to stop and look at many fascinating things along the way. But Carol appeared to be in a hurry, because she repeatedly turned and urged Julia to walk faster.

The following Saturday, I saw Carol and Julia out walking again. This time, Julia was in the lead and Carol was following, When Julia stopped to pick up a leaf or pebble, Carol stopped to admire it with her. The tempo of the outing was relaxed and pleasant, as if they had all the time in the world. It was beautiful to see an adult lovingly reinforce a child's natural appreciation of nature.

Several days later, I saw Carol and made a point of telling her how touched I'd been to see her walking with

Julia. I mentioned how different their walk had seemed from the weekday morning when they'd been hurrying along together. Carol said, "Oh, the first time you saw us, we were on what I call a 'time hike.' We were late for nursery school, and because Julia doesn't understand time like we do, she can't see any reason to rush.

"I don't want Julia to lose her ability to relax and enjoy things as she grows up, so on Saturday mornings we go on what I call 'being walks.' We go where Julia wants, and we pick up leaves, look at insects, and spend as much time enjoying nature as she likes."

Go for a walk with a child. Encourage their sense of wonder and share the delight of discovery.

EIGHTEEN

"*A* *joy shared is a joy doubled.*"

—GOETHE

When we share the outdoors with others, we receive much more than we give. Sharing intensifies our own, inner experiences. Enjoying nature with others reveals the aspects of the outdoors that we love most. Sharing nature's serenity and joy with others, we absorb the same qualities in increased measure ourselves.

Don't be concerned if you don't know much about natural history; the most important thing to communicate is your love and appreciation. Many nature games

Listening to Nature   **53**

are fun, and provide a structure that gives people new, focused experiences of nature. Often, a planned activity breaks the ice and helps people share more easily.

A game that everyone enjoys, whether child or adult, is "Meet A Tree." Take a friend to a forested area and blindfold them. Guide them to a tree. Let them "get to know the tree" by feeling its bark, its branches and leaves, looking for unique features. Walk your friend back to the starting place and remove the blindfold. Let them try to pick out "their" tree from all the others in the forest.

Make sure "their" tree doesn't have thorns or any harmful plants growing on it!

This activity and many others are described in my book, *Sharing Nature with Children,* in its sequel, *Sharing Nature Awareness,* and in similar environmental education resources.

NINETEEN

"*N*othing is so contagious as enthusiasm . . . it is the genius of sincerity, and truth accomplishes no victories without it."

—BULWER-LYTTON

The more we ourselves experience joy in nature, the better we can share that joy with others. Before sharing, use one of the activities in this book to tune into nature more deeply and experience its joy for yourself. You'll then have much more to offer others.

TWENTY

"*There must be the . . .
generating force of love
behind every effort destined to be
successful.*"

—HENRY DAVID THOREAU

Try this experiment: for one whole day, focus your attention on expressing love in everything you do, say, write or create. Carefully note the ways in which your experiences on this day differ from your normal day.

J. Donald Walters, in his book, *Education for Life,** has proposed this definition for maturity: "an ability to relate to others' realities, and not only to one's own." Love is what enables us to do this effortlessly. When we work with a spirit of love, we more fully understand people and their needs. And when there is harmony, so much more can be accomplished.

* Crystal Clarity, Publishers, 1986

TWENTY-ONE

"No matter how wet and cold you are, you're always warm and dry on the inside."

—WOODSMAN'S ADAGE

John Muir's way of keeping his contentment even under severe conditions was to lose himself in the wonder of the scene. Physical discomfort fled before his ability to find joy in the most fearsome, dangerous circumstances. Muir's ability to switch his attention from the cold and wet of a winter day to the beauty of a mountain snowstorm proved useful to me during a camping trip high in the Sierra Nevada mountains.

While we were loading the car, one of the ladies in our group told me she didn't have a sleeping bag, so I gave her mine and decided I'd experiment with a survival scheme I'd learned from a friend who claimed that plastic bags are very effective at trapping body heat. I was busy checking people's gear, so I asked someone to bring along two large, plastic refuse bags from the kitchen.

When the evening campfire had died to scarlet embers, we retired for the night. I pulled out the plastic bags and noticed they were just a little small! My fears were realized when, after tucking my feet and legs in, I found that the leg-bag came up only to my thighs; and the bag I pulled over my head came down only to my stomach. Even curled up tightly, I couldn't get the bags to overlap—no matter how I scrunched myself, there was always a good ten inches of open area.

I was in for a long, cold night, because we were above 7000 feet altitude. But by reminding myself, over and over, to "gaze at the wonder of the scene," I was able to make the best of an uncomfortable situation. In fact, I actually began to enjoy my predicament, watching the ever-so-slowly revolving night sky, the shooting stars, and listening to the wind blowing across the glacier-carved plateau.

TWENTY-TWO

"If the doors of perception were cleansed, everything would be seen as it is, infinite."

—WILLIAM BLAKE

When he was a young boy, George Washington Carver said, "Most people look, but they don't see."

When you visit a particularly beautiful place in the wild, or when you're just walking near your home and a beautiful flower or tree draws your attention, stop for a moment and spend a little time enjoying the moment. When restless thoughts come, such as "I should be hurrying along," ignore them for as long as possible. Bring your mind back to the moment of communion.

TWENTY-THREE

"*Never a day passes but that I do myself the honor to commune with some of nature's varied forms.*"

—GEORGE WASHINGTON CARVER

Tuning into Nature: Find a quiet place of natural beauty. Calm yourself by concentrating on your breath and feeling the power of life moving through you with each cycle of inhalation and exhalation.

Gradually expand your awareness beyond the breath, until you can sense the same flowing power of life in the things around you. Choose something of your surroundings to focus on: a tree, rock or blade of grass.

Feel the essence of life in that form of nature; then close your eyes and feel the same essence within yourself.

Open your eyes, and see how that essence fits into the whole: the forest, the mountain, the area, the earth. Enjoy the harmony of the many forms of life.

Feel your oneness with all life.

Walk slowly for a while, continually keeping awareness of your unity with all life.

TWENTY-FOUR

"Now this is what we believe.
The Mother of us all is
Earth.
The Father is the Sun.
The Grandfather is the Creator
Who bathed us with his mind
And gave life to all things.
The Brother is the
beasts and trees.
The Sister is that with wings.
We are the children of
Earth
And do it no harm in any way.
Nor do we offend the Sun
By not greeting it at dawn.
We praise our
Grandfather for his creation.
We share the same
breath together—
The beasts, the trees,
the birds, the man."

—NANCY WOOD (TAOS INDIANS)

Repeating the Indian prayer that follows here will help
you remember that the earth is alive, and that all creatures deserve equal love and respect. Feelings of respect
lead to gratitude; a grateful heart enables us to be ever
more humbly in sympathy with other creatures. Humility
allows us to see life in proper proportion, understanding
that our human desires should be tempered with willing-
ness to defer to the needs of other living things. The
environmental crisis today can be traced directly to lack
of proper respect and humility.

When you need to cut down a tree or remove a plant
from your garden, reflect on this prayer:

> *We know that we all are children of the same*
> *Mother Earth, of our Father Sun. But we also*
> *know that one life must sometime give way to*
> *another, so that the one great life of all may*
> *continue unbroken. So we ask your permis-*
> *sion, we obtain your consent to this killing.*

FRANK WATERS

Listening to Nature   **65**

TWENTY-FIVE

"*Holy Earth Mother, the trees and all nature are witnesses of your thoughts and deeds.*"

—WINNEBAGO INDIANS

John Muir said, "Every natural object is a conductor of divinity." Muir believed in a divine presence that is expressed in everything. Go for a walk, silently repeating this Winnebago prayer of reverence for the earth and its Creator. When an animal, plant, rock, or a beautiful scene draws your attention, stop, and silently offer thanks for the joy and beauty you feel.

You can use the following prayer similarly:

> *I feel Thy presence in this landscape which draws my heart so close to Thee.*
>
> Hazrat Inayat Khan

TWENTY-SIX

"The first peace, which is the
most important, is that
which comes within the souls of
people when they
realize their relationship, their
oneness, with the
universe and all its powers, and
when they realize that
at the center of the universe dwells
the Great Spirit, and
that this center is really
everywhere, it is
within each of us."

—BLACK ELK

TWENTY-SEVEN

Nature Channels Song

"Birds sing of freedom as they
soar lightly on the air.
So may our hearts soar, high above
all curbs and care.

Trees, standing firm,
hold the secret of inner power.
Give us, when tested,
strength to endure.
Mountains, remote
and still, hint at higher worlds unseen.
So may our lives be: soaring and
serene.

Rivers seek passage,
unhindered by rock or tree.
So may our lives flow,
steadfast toward the sea!

Mother, we thank you, your joy
shines in everything!
Open these channels, that the
world once more may sing."

—J. DONALD WALTERS

Many years ago there lived in a small village, in a country far away, a very wise and respected sage. He was often asked by visitors how he had become so wise. "Where did you study? Who was your teacher?" they asked. On one occasion the old man replied, "To this day, I have many teachers, and my studies continue in the woods and mountains that surround my village." Then his face became radiant and content. Gazing up at the forested slopes of the mountains, he softly added, "I have learned many valuable lessons there."

"The rocks were among my first teachers. From them I have learned how to sit and be still. Once I did this, I began to notice everything around me in a new way. An oak tree taught me the difference one life can make: I saw how this oak and its brethren warmed the cold winter and made the summer's heat more pleasant; how the forest animals came to the tree for shelter, food and comfort. Since then I have tried to live for others."

Like the sage in the story, we can learn valuable lessons from nature. Nature is an expression of God; or, if you prefer, of the creative force and intelligence in the universe. Since we are created by the same power as nature, we can use nature as a mirror in which to reflect on truths about ourselves.

You can also sing "Nature Channels" as a way to show your appreciation of the beauty and uniqueness of the many expressions of nature. (To obtain the sheet music, see the Index to Quotations.)

*"Those who have the humility of
a child may find again
the key to reverence for, and
kinship with, all life."*

—J. Allen Boone

Saint Francis Prayer

"*Lord, make me an instrument*
of Thy peace.
Where there is hatred,
let me sow love;
Where there is injury, pardon;
Where there is doubt, faith;
Where there is despair, hope;
Where there is darkness, light;
Where there is sadness, joy.

O Divine Master, grant that I may
not so much seek
To be consoled, as to console,
To be understood, as
to understand,
To be loved, as to love.
For it is in giving that we receive,
It is in pardoning, that
we are pardoned,
It is in dying to self
that we are born to eternal life."

—SAINT FRANCIS OF ASSISI

Saint Francis felt great love for plants, animals, and even the natural elements, and was deeply disturbed when he saw them handled disrespectfully. Once, Francis offered a woodcutter his own small daily portion of food if the woodcutter would only spare one branch of the tree, so that it might grow back again.

On another occasion, Francis met a farmer carrying a sheep to market and exchanged the cloak on his back for the sheep, so that it might live.

Many times, animals followed Francis for miles as he wandered the roads and hillside paths of his native Umbria. Sometimes they even entered buildings with him, because they were so powerfully drawn by his love.

At a mountain hermitage on Mount Subasio, near Assisi, is located one of several sites where Saint Francis is said to have preached to the birds. When I visited Mount Subasio, the thought came, "What was the secret of Francis's love of nature and of his ability to converse with the animals?" The answer came very clearly: "Francis could feel his oneness with others and with nature because he never thought of himself."

When we aren't thinking about ourselves, we are more able to feel our unity with others. The Saint Francis Prayer is a wonderful meditation for turning our focus away from ourselves, and to begin to reach out to those around us.

In the morning and before going to sleep at night, repeat the prayer several times. Memorize it, so that you can repeat it mentally at appropriate moments during the day.

THIRTY

"*I care to live only to entice
people to look at
nature's loveliness. My own special
self is nothing. [I want
to be] like a flake of glass through
which light passes.*"

—JOHN MUIR

John Muir, the Scottish-born naturalist, was one of North America's greatest conservationists. Seventy years since his passing, his writings on nature and the tremendous joy he felt in the natural world still inspire people and remind us of the vital message nature has for our lives.

Muir's great love for nature was intensified by his ability to forget himself completely, totally immersing himself in the beauty of his surroundings. Often Muir would become so absorbed in the natural world that he would be barely conscious of the passage of time. Sometimes he would lose consciousness of his own separate existence entirely, and feel himself merging with the totality of nature.

Muir wonderfully exemplified the power of true humility—not meekness or smallness, but an ability to forget his own small self completely and absorb himself in the joy of nature. This quality is perhaps the most necessary of all for deepening our appreciation of nature, because when we forget ourselves, we are able to receive the spirit of the world around us.

Self-forgetfulness gives birth to the many other qualities we need in order to develop an active environmental ethic. Humility opens the inner doorway to love, because it is only the barriers of our self-interest that separate us from the rest of life. In absorption in what we love, our thoughts become quiet; thus love brings a wonderful poise and serenity into our lives.

Reverence for life is the result of love, because in love we begin to feel ourselves in everything around us. Our actions toward other beings become more caring, because we understand that, in harming others, we are harming ourselves. Thus, a natural outgrowth of the inner fulfilment we feel is a desire to share and to selflessly serve the source of our inspiration.

THIRTY-ONE

"Walk away quietly in any direction and taste the freedom of the mountaineer . . .

Climb the mountains and get their good tidings. Nature's peace will flow into you as sunshine flows into trees. The winds will blow their own freshness into you, and the storms their energy, while cares will drop off like autumn leaves."

—JOHN MUIR

How to Get the Most Out of This Book

RECALL A TIME when you were out in nature and "something special" happened. Perhaps you found an unusually beautiful flower, or you witnessed one of nature's rare events, such as a snow avalanche, or a thunderstorm. You may have experienced on that occasion, perhaps for the first time, a deep feeling of oneness with all life. Whatever the factors were, the moment was precious, and the hope of having another such experience is what draws you back to nature.

Can we really *expect* to experience one of those "rare moments" every time we go out into nature? That's not as unreasonable as it may sound, for nature is *full* of those rare moments. The only thing that prevents us from being aware of them is our own frame of mind, which alone keeps us from noticing and enjoying them.

When we go into nature, it should be as Thoreau said, with "abandonment, and childlike mirthfulness." Only in a spirit of complete attentiveness and wonder can we be freely receptive to nature's inspirations.

Sensitively tuning into nature can bring us rejuvenating and uplifting experiences, which in turn inspire us to noble aspirations and actions. My purpose in writing this book has been to help you to prepare yourself to be more open to such experiences. I have personally used the activities in this book, and I know that they can give you such experiences. When I want to get into a state of mind to receive inspiration from nature, I'll do two or more of them in succession. To illustrate how you, too, can use them to get inspiration, let me share a couple of stories from my own experience. One spring afternoon, high in the Sierra Nevada mountains, I sat peacefully after enjoying the Stillness Meditation. I was doing the Still Hunting activity when, just thirty feet away, two young pine martens poked their heads out of their den. (Pine martens are weasels, about the size of a small domestic cat. They have long bushy tails and are extremely fast and elusive.) The martens were only a couple of months old and very inquisitive. At first they were very slow and cautious in venturing forth from the safety of their den; but soon they lost all fear and began wrestling and chasing each other. Now and then, they'd stop to investigate a new and mysterious object in their surroundings.

One of them finally noticed me, and with curiosity overcoming its native caution, came forward to find out what I was. The other young marten followed, stopped, and gazed intently at me from just a few feet away. Meanwhile, the braver and more inquisitive one came right up and began sniffing my left leg.

Mother, who apparently had been busy elsewhere, came back at this moment and was greatly alarmed to see her offspring examining me so closely. She rushed forward, barked a *come home at once!*, and herded her two frightened children into the den.

I was profoundly moved by the innocent trust of those two young pine martens, and by the joy I felt when looking into their beautiful, curious eyes. I'm sure I was the first human they had seen. Their lack of fear deeply touched my heart and made our meeting all the more memorable. I would never have felt such a bond with the martens—or probably even seen them—had I not stopped and sat quietly for a long time. My use of the activities had helped me remain quietly attentive.

On another occasion, not long ago, I spent some time enjoying the view from the rim of the Grand Canyon. After an hour or so, I began to feel restless and to think about returning to my car. Yet, because I don't have many

opportunities to visit the Grand Canyon, I wanted to make the most of my time there.

I did several of the activities from *Listening to Nature,* one after another, to bring my mind back to enjoy the moment and to tune into the special, inspiring mood of the Canyon. I remember how, on that day, I especially enjoyed Expanding Circles, and also the poem, "My heart is tuned to the quietness that the stillness of nature inspires," because of the expansiveness and serenity of the view across the Canyon. Because those activities worked so well, I was able to spend several hours of rich contemplation at the Canyon's edge—an experience I would have missed, had I succumbed to my first temptation to get up and leave. My own increased receptivity and concentration made all the difference.

The Index to Activities will help you locate the activities you may wish to use. If you decide to use several of the activities in succession to enhance your enjoyment of a natural place, I suggest you use them in this order:

Begin with the Stillness Meditation or Expanding Circles, because they will calm your mind and make it receptive. Calmness intensifies the practice of the other activities.

Still Hunting, Tuning into Nature, and silently repeating inspiring quotations, or poems like "The Birds of the Air," are good follow-up activities, because it's easy and appropriate to do them while remaining seated. (If you hear birds nearby, you might try the bird calling activity.)

When you feel like getting up and moving around, try activities like Walking and Feeling Yourself in All, or silently repeat the Navajo poem, "With beauty all around me . . ."

These are merely suggestions, based on my own experiences. Most important of all, please use these activities and quotations in the ways that most inspire you.

INDEX TO ACTIVITIES

INDEX TO QUOTATIONS

(alphabetical by author)

Cornell (Day 6)—Music for Joseph Cornell's "The Birds of the Air" is available from Dawn Publications. Send $1 plus self-addressed, stamped envelope. Or, order from Exley Publications by sending £1 with a stamped, addressed envelope.

Cornell (Day 10)—Joseph Cornell

Goethe (Day 18)—Johann Wolfgang von Goethe

Khan (Day 8)—from *Nature Meditations* by Hazrat Inayat Khan. Sufi Order Publications

Khan (Day 25)—from *Nature Meditations* by Hazrat Inayat Khan. Sufi Order Publications

Lao Tzu (Day 11)

Muir (Day 12)—from *Son to the Wilderness : A Life of John Muir* by Linnie Marsh Wolfe. Alfred A. Knopf. 1945

Muir (Day 14)—from *John of the Mountains* edited by Linnie Marsh Wolfe. Copyright 1954 by Wanda Muir Hanna. Copyright © renewed 1966 by John Muir Hanna and Ralph Eugene Wolfe. Reprinted by permission of Houghton Mifflin Co.

Muir (Day 30)—from *Son to the Wilderness : A Life of John Muir* by Linnie Marsh Wolfe. Alfred A. Knopf. 1945

Muir (Day 31)—from *The Wilderness World of John Muir* edited by Edwin Teale. Copyright 1954 by Edwin W. Teale. Copyright © renewed 1966 by Nellie D. Teale. Reprinted by permission of Houghton Mifflin Co.

Navajo (Day 5)—from *American Indian Poetry* edited by George W. Cronyn. Liveright/W.W. Norton Co.

Olson (Day 7)—from *Reflections from the North Country* by Sigurd Olson. Alfred A. Knopf. 1976

St. Francis of Assisi (Day 29)

Tanaka Shozo (Day 3)—from *Ox Against the Storm* by Kenneth Strong. Univ. of British Columbia Press. 1977

Thoreau (Day 9)—from *The Writings of Henry David Thoreau,* edited by Bradford Torry and Francis H. Allen. Houghton Mifflin Co. 1906

Thoreau (Day 20)—from *The Writings of Henry David Thoreau,* edited by Bradford Torry and Francis H. Allen. Houghton Mifflin Co. 1906

Walters (Day 27)—from *Ring, Bluebell, Ring!* by J. Donald Walters. Music for "Nature Channels Song" is available from Dawn Publications. Send $1 plus self-addressed, stamped envelope. Or, order from Exley Publications by sending £1 with a stamped, addressed envelope.

Waters (Day 24)—from *The Man Who Killed the Deer* by Frank Waters. Ohio University Press

Whitman (Day 4)—from *Leaves of Grass* by Walt Whitman. H.W. Wilson Co.

Winnebago Indians (Day 25)

Wood (Day 24)—from *Many Winters* by Nancy Wood. Doubleday & Co. 1974

Woodsman's adage (Day 21)

Publishers' Note: Every effort has been made to locate the copyright holders of the material quoted in the text. Omissions brought to our attention will be credited in subsequent printings. Grateful acknowledgment is made to those publishers who asked that their ownership be noted in this index.

PHOTOGRAPHIC NOTES

John Hendrickson, who has provided all but two of the photographs in this book, is a widely-known nature photographer whose work has appeared in many publications and museums.* John travels extensively throughout the world to do freelance photography, give lectures and conduct photo exhibitions. He also is Resident Director of Woodleaf Outdoor School in northern California.

John is noted for his ability to convey both creative artistry and biological knowledge through his photographs. He offers the following thoughts on how he does this:

"Although equipment quality and technical execution are important in nature photography, I firmly believe that to become a better nature photographer, one must first become a better naturalist. When I am out in nature—walking, looking and sensing for a photograph—I usually begin with a 'tuning in' process. Where there is water, I might touch it, splash my face and arms, or even jump in. I sometimes pick up leaves and crinkle them, smell their fragrance and rub them over my skin. Often I will sit, stretching, watching and relaxing for up to an hour before I begin to take photographs. This process helps me feel a part of nature, that nature is not merely "out there," but is within me as well. It also helps me feel what I want to say and express.

"When photographing birds, I often sit waiting for hours, sometimes days, in blinds. Many people marvel at my patience, but to be honest, I don't see it as an ordeal. I enjoy sitting alone, in a blind, watching. This time helps me reflect and focus. I've learned more while sitting in

blinds than I ever did at a school desk. My knowledge as a naturalist comes firsthand, and it is the most valuable photographic tool I possess.

"While working on the photographs for this book, I often read the text to help me get a photograph that would match the spirit of the words. What a joy it was to feel that spirit matching the spirit of the land! While studying a scene, several quotations often floated through my mind. The text seemed to work its way into me, just as nature often does. Clearly, the writings deepened my sensitivity and helped my photography.

"My photographs in this book were shot with a Canon F-1 35mm camera, using Kodachrome 64 film and a variety of lenses ranging from 28mm to 500mm. I prefer to use 35mm equipment because it enables me to travel light, freeing my attention to focus on what's around me, rather than on what I'm carrying. I do, however, consider a sturdy tripod to be essential. I rarely use filters of any kind—I used none for this book—because I believe that natural light offers the best environment for expressing my impressions accurately.

"Although I try to record the substance and spirit of each moment, the photographs are certainly no substitute for the real thing. They simply cannot replace the chill of morning, the smell of fresh rain, the crackle of leaves underfoot, or the exhilaration of being close to a wild animal. To have the total experience, you must go there yourself. Clearly, we must preserve the world's remaining wilderness areas, not only for the health of our planet, but for our own spiritual and mental health as well."

---

* The photographs for days 10 and 29 were taken by Joseph Cornell.

EDUCATION FOR LIFE
WORKSHOPS

Would you like to deepen your awareness of nature, or share nature's beauty and mystery with the children in your life? You can easily learn how, in workshops specially developed by Joseph Cornell.

Several times each year, Mr. Cornell offers his nature awareness workshop for adults. Based on the concepts underlying this book, this workshop gives you guided nature awareness experiences as well as additional tools that you can use on your own.

If you want to work with children, Mr. Cornell has developed a workshop based on his classic book, *Sharing Nature with Children.* Whether your own background in nature is vast or limited, you'll come away with literally hundreds of ideas for more effective sharing. The *Sharing Nature with Children* workshop is offered year-round, with leaders personally trained by Joseph Cornell.

These are two of the workshops offered by the Education for Life Foundation. Other offerings include: Supportive Leadership for Principals and Lead Teachers; The Discipline Workshop; Self-Worth Seminar Series—a training program designed for teachers and parents to help children see themselves as worthwhile and valuable individuals. For more information, contact: Education for Life Foundation, 14618 Tyler Foote Road, Nevada City, California 95959; Telephone (916) 292-3775.

The Education for Life Foundation was established to promote educational programs that combine both academic excellence and character development in children. The Foundation views success not only as outward achievement, but as inner strength and maturity. The Education for Life Core School, founded in 1970, provides the framework for the Foundation's work. In addition to offering workshops, the Foundation also serves as consultant for school districts wishing to promote Education for Life principles in their classrooms.

My deepest thanks to J. Donald Walters for his example of wisdom and joy, and because it was his book, The *Secret of Happiness** that gave me the initial inspiration for this book.

I am also very grateful to George Beinhorn, Christy Dixon, Sheila Rush, Asha Praver, Peter MacDow, Rich McCord, Jim Van Cleave and numerous others who have given invaluable suggestions.

Lastly, I want to express my thanks and appreciation to Anandi, my wife, for her support while writing this book, and also for her insights and ability to help me clarify my ideas.

---

* Crystal Clarity, Publishers, 1987
